W9-CPE-223

About Keep Iowa Beautiful

Governor Robert D. Ray and other dedicated individuals and organizations recognize that a clean, attractive state is an important component of our Iowa environment and quality of life here in the Heartland. All of us who live here, and the many visitors who come to share our state's beauty and bounty, recognize the commitment of those who have joined together to Keep Iowa Beautiful.

Keep Iowa Beautiful works as a private charitable organization supporting and working for a cleaner and more attractive state. The following efforts touch all of our lives by making Iowa a better place to live:

- Countryside/community/neighborhood enhancement assistance through efforts such as Hometown Pride.
- Reduction in litter and illegal dumping.
- Increasing levels of recycling and waste reduction.
- Public awareness and education efforts empowering Iowans to be active in improving the quality of the state.
- Facilitating community enhancement projects through financial grants and Diamond Vogel paint grants.
- Working with schools, citizens and educators to increase the levels and quality of service learning in our schools.
- Increasing the utilization of K -12 education programs developed for teachers, e.g., Teachers Going Green and the Clean and Green curriculum.

Robert D. Ray

A photographic journey of the life and travels
of former Governor of Iowa Robert D. Ray

Pioneer Communications, Printer, Jim Slife, CEO
Mark Lunde, Editor
Pat Fultz, Fultz Design, Designer

First printing February 2013, Printed in U.S.A.
ISBN: 978-1-934816-29-5 Hard Cover
ISBN: 978-1-934816-30-1 Soft Cover

Robert D. Kay

Dear Friends:

I have been privileged to serve the people of Iowa in a number of capacities during my life.

One of my proudest achievements was serving as Co-Founder and Chairman of Keep Iowa Beautiful (KIB) in 2000. I continue to serve on the Board of Directors along with other dedicated Iowans. Building beautiful communities in which our citizens live, work and raise a family continues to be the goal of Keep Iowa Beautiful.

For many years, I have had a passion to capture Iowa and the world through photography. During many of my travels, I had my camera with me and took numerous photos of the people, places and communities where they lived. As Billie and I looked through the albums and boxes of photos from our travels over the years, we discovered we also had gathered photos taken by others as we traveled the world from Iowa to the Great Wall of China.

We are pleased and honored to share some of these photos with you. We hope you enjoy this geographical tour of Iowa and the world through a camera. Your purchase of this book is greatly appreciated. All proceeds go to Keep Iowa Beautiful for their many programs that enhance our state.

Thank you for your support.

Sincerely,

Robert D. Ray

Robert D. Ray

Contents

World Traveler 80

Robert D. Ray

Few names in Iowa history are as instantly recognizable as Robert D. Ray.

He was born in Des Moines in 1928, served in the U.S. Army and graduated from Drake University with a business degree in 1952 and a law degree in 1954. He served as a law and reading clerk for the Iowa State Senate and became a respected and successful Iowa trial lawyer. In 1963 he was the Iowa Republican state chair, Chairman of the Republican State Central Committee and a member of the Republican National Committee, and he's credited with rebuilding the party after its heavy losses in 1964. *Time* named Ray one of "America's Young Leaders" in 1974 and in 2000 he was named "Most Influential Iowan" by the *New York Times.*

Bob Ray was elected Governor of Iowa for a then-unprecedented five terms beginning in 1968. During his time in office, he was chairman of the National Governors Association, the Midwest Governors Association, the Education Commission of the States, and he was president of the Council of State Governments. In 1979, he was appointed a member of the U.S. delegation to the Special United Nations Conference on Refugees in Geneva, Switzerland.

In the late 1970s, Governor Ray became a worldwide leader in the humanitarian resettlement of refugees from Laos, Cambodia, Thailand and Vietnam, helping them to relocate, find jobs and start new lives in Iowa. "I didn't think we could just sit idly by and say, let those people die. We wouldn't want the rest of the world to say that about us if we were in the same situation."

A problem developed with the Thai Dam, because the U.S. State Department would not allow a large group of refugees to settle in one location. Governor Ray traveled to the White House and State Department and prevailed on President Gerald Ford and Secretary of State Henry Kissinger to make an exception. Finally, Thai Dam were invited to resettle in Iowa in significant numbers.

While governor, Bob Ray issued executive orders promoting civil rights, energy conservation and paperwork reduction, as well as establishing the Governor's Economy Committee, the Iowa Council of Children, the Task Force on Government Ethics, the Science Advisory Council, the Iowa High Technology Commission and the Iowa Natural Heritage Foundation. Ray signed legislation establishing the Iowa Commission on the Status of Women and was a strong advocate on the nickel deposit on aluminum cans to help keep our streets and roadsides cleaner and more attractive.

Following his 14 years as Governor of Iowa, Ray became President and Chief Executive Officer of Life Investors, Inc., now known as AEGON Inc. Following that, he served as President and CEO of Blue Cross and Blue Shield of Iowa, now Wellmark. He was Chairman of the Board of Trustees and later President of Drake University. He also filled a term as Mayor of Des Moines. Ray has been actively involved in national health care issues, serving as co-chair of the National Leadership Coalition on Health Care, a member of the U.S. Surgeon General's Task Force on Mental Health and the Carter Center's Mental Health Advisory Board. He chaired the Advisory Committee on Rural Health for Congress and served on the President's Commission on Consumer Protection and Quality in the Health Care Industry. Ray also helped create the Iowa Character Counts program and the program to which this book is dedicated, Keep Iowa Beautiful.

Public Servant

A lawyer, governor, U.S. Delegate, mayor—the list goes on and on. Robert D. Ray is a man who has dedicated his career to making life better for individuals, especially the people of Iowa.

His tireless efforts on issues of environment, human rights, the economy and public health will benefit our state for years to come. He is without question one of the most beloved citizens the state of Iowa has ever known.

Left: Governor Ray and Iowa First Lady Billie on one of their many visits on behalf of Iowa to our nation's capitol.

Above: Ray signs a proclamation in the governor's office.

Below: Former First Lady Betty Ford and former Governor Ray address a campaign rally for Congressman Jim Leach.

Right: Former Governor Ray shares a moment with Congressman Jim Leach.

IOWA and JIM LEAC
WELCOME
BETTY
FORD and
GOVERNOR
RAY

Celebrating historical moments in Iowa and the life of Robert D. Ray

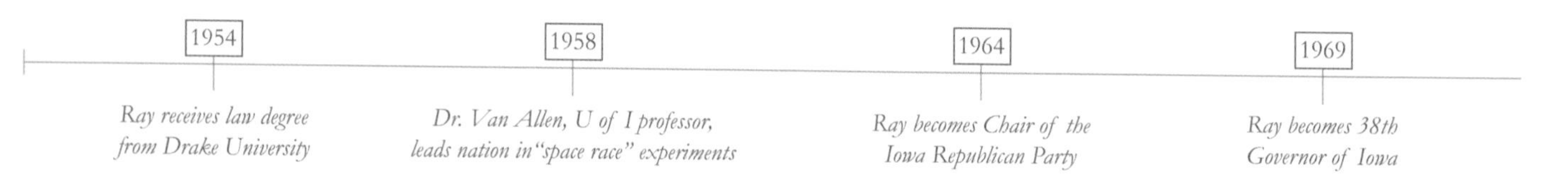
1954
Ray receives law degree from Drake University
1958
Dr. Van Allen, U of I professor, leads nation in "space race" experiments
1964
Ray becomes Chair of the Iowa Republican Party
1969
Ray becomes 38th Governor of Iowa

Left: Ray with former Secretary of State Henry Kissinger.

Below: Ray meeting with members of his staff. Long days, long meetings!

Left: Ray speaking at a Governor's Conference.

Right: The governor with former President Richard Nixon.

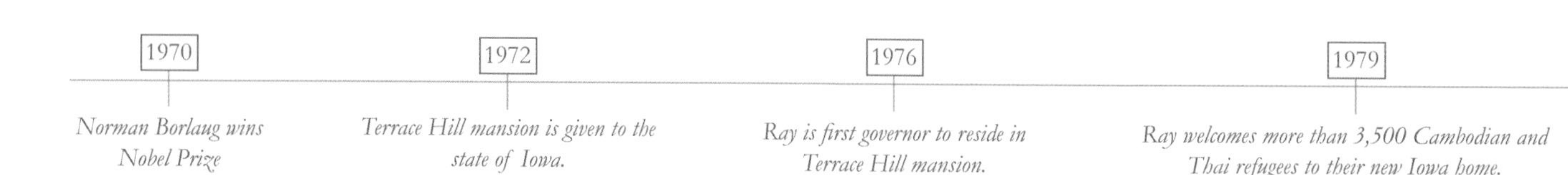

1970
Norman Borlaug wins Nobel Prize
1972
Terrace Hill mansion is given to the state of Iowa.
1976
Ray is first governor to reside in Terrace Hill mansion.
1979
Ray welcomes more than 3,500 Cambodian and Thai refugees to their new Iowa home.

Below: Ray on the set with Sylvester Stallone during the making of the movie, *F.I.S.T.*, in Dubuque, Iowa.

Right: Governor Ray delivering one of many State of the State addresses to the Iowa General Assembly.

1979	1983	1984	1985
Ray helps create Iowa Natural Heritage Foundation	*Ray becomes President and CEO of Life Investors, Inc.*	*Ray appointed as U.S. Delegate to the U.N.*	*Ray chairs the Ray Commission for the effectiveness of refugee programs*

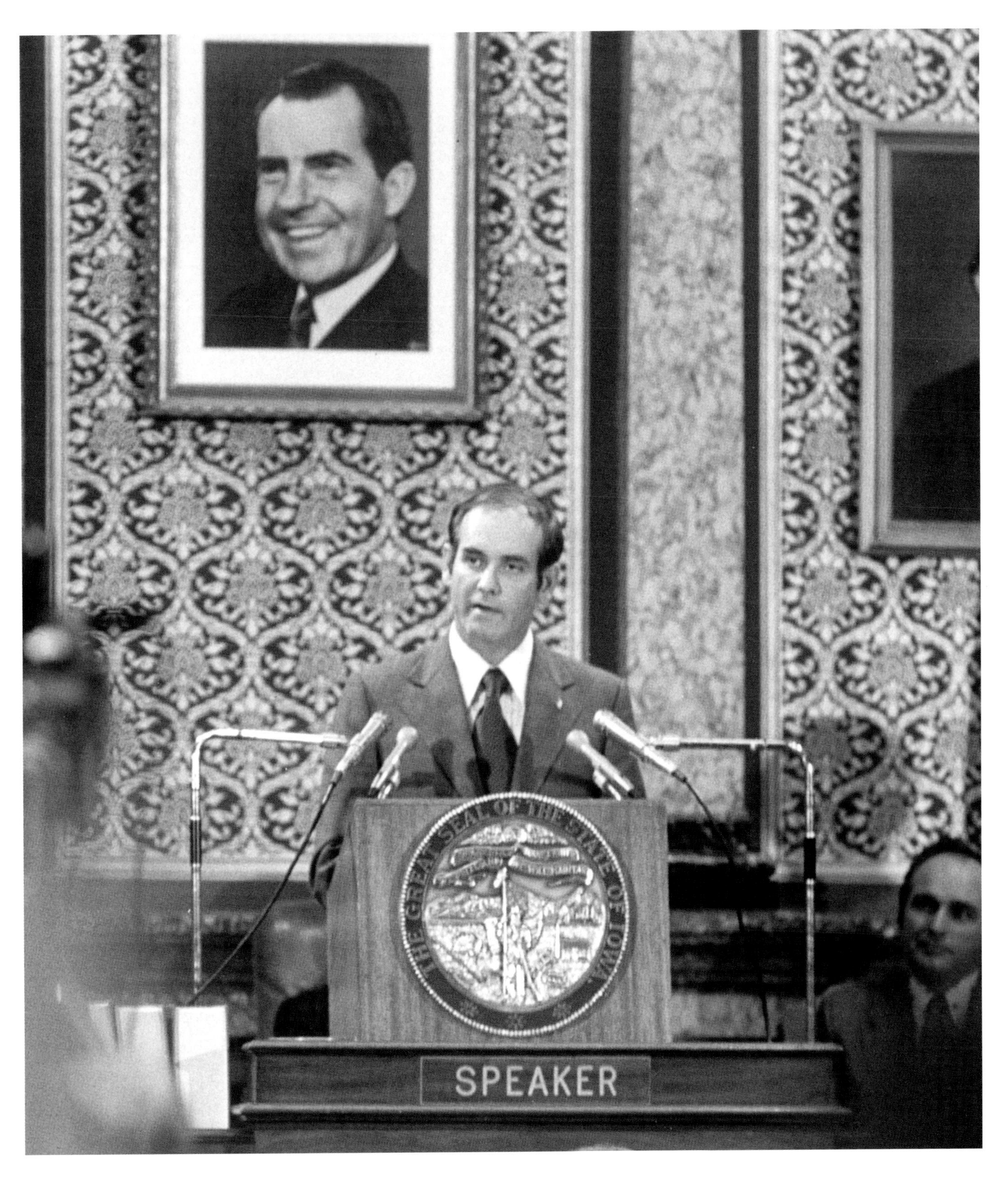
THE GREAT SEAL OF THE STATE OF IOWA
SPEAKER

Left: Ray speaking with former President Ronald Reagan and former First Lady Nancy Reagan.

Below: Governor Ray meets with former President Reagan, former Vice President George H.W. Bush and others in the Oval Office.

GEORGE BUSH

November 14, 2012

Dear Bob;

Greetings, old friend!

I see from this marvelous book that you continue to be very active in your great State of Iowa. Your fellow Hawkeyes are lucky to have one of their favorite sons still leading the charge on important matters. Certainly, Keeping Iowa Beautiful is a most worthy endeavor.

Your record of service will long be remembered; and this book -- and a look at your work through the lens of a camera -- is a great way to reflect your legacy. Congratulations!

With warmest regards and friendship,

G Bush

The Honorable Robert D. Ray
Keep Iowa Beautiful
Des Moines, IA 50309

ge Bush
George

UNITED STATES

Left: Ray speaking at the United Nations while a U.S. Delegate.

Above: Bob and Billie share a quiet conversation with former President Jimmy Carter.

Governor's
CHARITY
SHOW

Above: Governor Ray with then Lt. Governor Terry Branstad at the Iowa State Fair Governor's Charity Show. Who has the best hat?

Right: Governor Ray shares a laugh with Former President Gerald Ford in the Oval Office.

1988
Ray appointed to National Advisory Committee on Rural Health Care
1989
Ray hired as President and CEO of Blue Cross Blue Shield
1991
Ray chairs the Iowa Sesquicentennial Commission
1993
Famous floods of 1993

"I've had the pleasure of knowing Bob Ray since the late 1970s, when we were both serving as governors. Iowa is a better place because of his lifetime of public service, and his leadership with Keep Iowa Beautiful continues to build on that remarkable legacy. As you can see from this terrific collection of photographs from around the world, Bob makes friends wherever he goes—but his heart is always in Iowa."

Bill Clinton

Above: Governor Ray with former First Lady, U.S. Senator and Secretary of State Hillary Clinton.

Left and above: Bob Ray with President George W. Bush.

Below: Bob and Billie with Governor Terry Branstad and former U.S. Senator Bob Dole.

Right: Ray with Senator Bob Dole from our neighbor state of Kansas.

GOVERNOR RAY

LEADERSHIP

Governor Ray proved his persuasiveness, responsibility and reliability as he rose in public life. Loyalty is one of the keys to his success, and he frequently is consulted by Republican party leaders, including National Chairman Robert Dole (above).

Confident leader with confidence in Iowa and Iowans

GOVERNOR RAY

Friends of Governor Ray, Rand Petersen, Treasurer.

I LIKE BOB RAY THE GOVERNOR

Credit: Iowa Historical Society

1997	1998	1999	2000
Ray chairs the Institute for Character Development	*Ray serves as president of Drake University*	*Ray serves as interim mayor for Des Moines*	*Ray helps create Keep Iowa Beautiful*

ditorial pages, 515-284-8540

Sunday Register

THE FORUM

"When voters pulled the lever for Bob Ray, they were voting for a team. People voted for Bob and Billie."

'Governor': An Iowa love story

By RICHARD DOAK

"Governor," an oral biography of former Gov. Robert Ray, mostly dwells on politics and government, as one might expect. It is also a terrific love story.

"... when voters pulled the lever for Bob Ray, they were voting for a team," Frosty Mitchell told biographer Jon Bowermaster. "People voted for Bob and Billie."

"I've always viewed them as one of the great love affairs I've been a firsthand observer to," said Verne Lawyer, Ray's former law partner.

Readers of "Governor" should by no means expect intimate details about Bob and Billie

GOVERNOR: An Oral Biography of Robert D. Ray by Jon Bowermaster. 336 pages. Iowa State University Press, $19.95.

Ray. The Rays guard their privacy far too much for that. But the warm story of a successful long-term marriage — the best kind of love story, after all — comes through in Bowermaster's interviews of friends, associates and the Rays themselves.

Dwelling on that love story here serves both to provide a glimpse of one part of the Ray success that hasn't been widely told, as well as to provide a sampler of Bowermaster's biographical technique.

Bob and Billie Ray had known each other in high school and from church. They married in 1951, after Ray had returned from Army service in Japan. He was a law student at Drake; Billie was a teacher.

After Ray graduated, the young couple went off on a low-budget lark to Europe with Jim and Joann Tyler. "They were very, very close," Joann Tyler recalled; "... he would often make a statement followed by, 'Isn't that so, Billie Lee?' or 'Don't you agree, Billie Lee?' He would often bounce things off her."

Here is Bob Ray telling of his decision to seek the Republican nomination for governor in 1968, when he would be the long-shot in a three-way primary:

"Billie really made the difference. She came to me one night, and she said, 'I see these people talking to you about running for governor. At first I saw you dismiss the idea and then I saw you, more lately, listen, like you're getting interested.' She said, 'I don't want you to run. I don't want you to get any deeper into politics,

Below: Former Mayor Bob Ray and members of the Des Moines City Council.

Right: Ray presenting a gift from Iowa to the King of Thailand.

Humanitarian

Indochina

Between 1975 and 1980, Governor Robert Ray provided global humanitarian leadership on behalf of refugees from Indochina. He was the only governor in America to answer the plea from the ethnic Thai Dam from Laos, who begged to be resettled together in one U.S. state in order to keep their language and customs intact. When the Vietnamese Boat People were facing death while fleeing on small, unseaworthy crafts in search of freedom, Governor Ray was the first political leader anywhere in the world to commit to rescuing these refugees. His letter to President Carter convinced the president to reopen America's doors, welcoming 168,000 new refugees a year. The Boat People were saved, thanks to Iowa's governor. Finally, after personally witnessing the horrific loss of life among Cambodian refugees who had suffered under the genocidal Khmer Rouge, Ray started Iowa SHARES (Iowa Sends Help to Aid Refugees and Starvation), which raised more than $600,000 to rush Iowa doctors and nurses with lifesaving food and medicine to the Thai-Cambodian border.

Written by

Ambassador Kenneth M. Quinn | President, World Food Prize

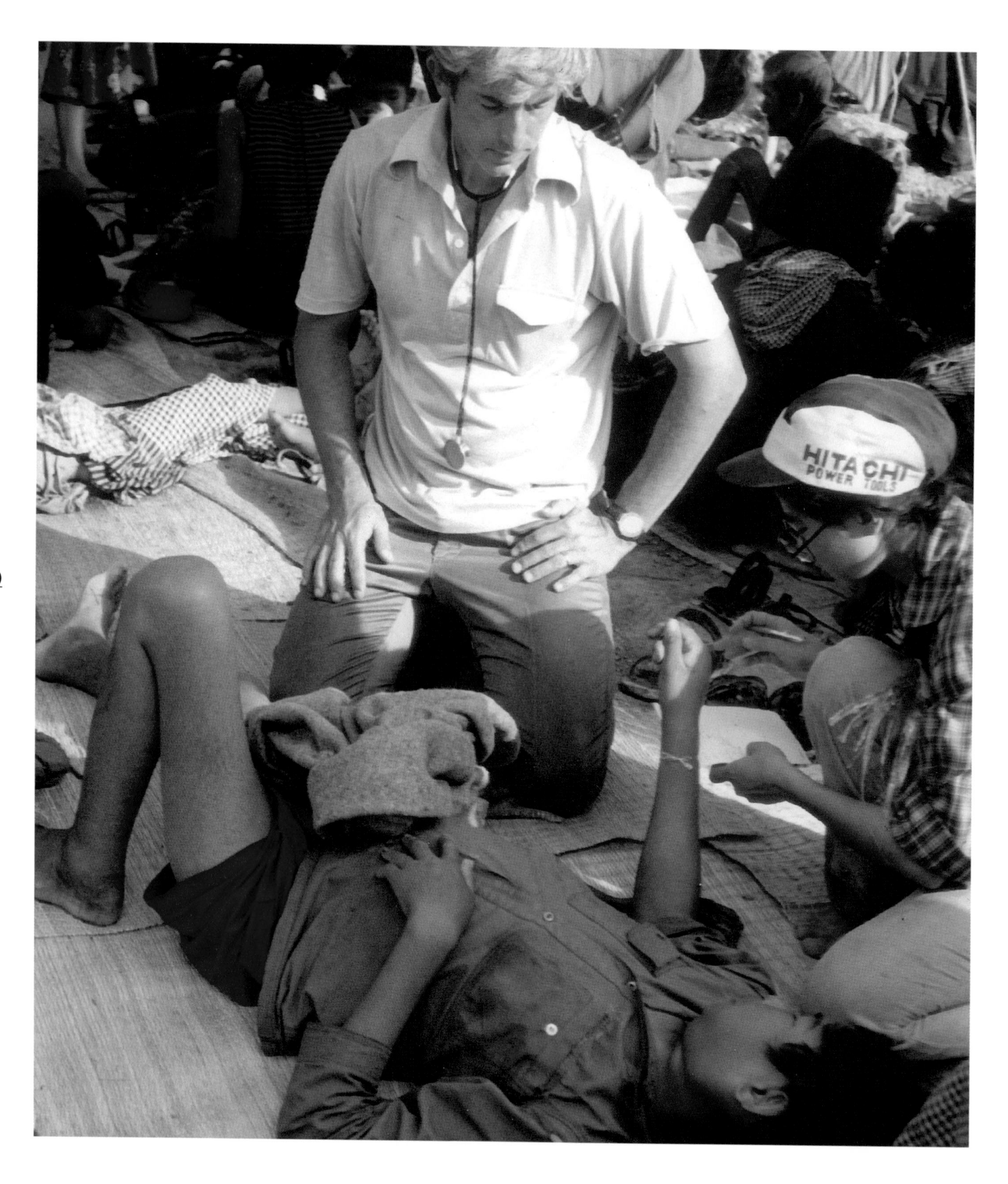
HITACHI
POWER TOOLS

"We were so moved by the horrible living conditions and constant danger these people were forced to live under that we knew we had to do everything in our power to help them leave. They deserved a better future. And we helped them find it—in Iowa."

Community Leader

In 2000, the *New York Times* called Bob Ray "The most influential Iowan" of his time. It was a title Bob would humbly wave off, however well deserved the distinction. After an illustrious political career like Bob's, some people might have been ready to put up their feet and relish in their successes. But Bob Ray chose a different path. His desire was to stay actively involved in the state of Iowa and continue to champion the issues he felt passionate about. His journey led him to become a CEO of two prominent insurance companies, president of a private university and an active member of numerous worldwide organizations. Today, you can still find Bob attending meetings for organizations that are near and dear to his heart.

Above: Former Governor Bob Ray and Billie Ray welcome Pope John Paul II on his historic visit to Iowa in 1979.

Above: Ray presenting an award to Olympic Gold Medal gymnast Shawn Johnson at the Character Counts awards ceremony.

Left: Bob and Billie Ray meeting with His Holiness Pope John Paul II at the Vatican on one of their many ambassador trips.

bert D Ray Dr

Left: Ray standing by the street sign for Robert D. Ray Drive, in front of Des Moines City Hall with the Iowa State Capitol in the background.

Above: Bob and Billie Ray were instrumental in the creation of the Chinese Cultural Center of Ames.

Left: Bob and Billie with Iowa State University Architecture Professor Dr. Paul Y. Shao, board member of the Chinese Cultural Center of Ames.

Right: As President of Drake University, Ray meets with prominent Des Moines businessman Marvin Pomerantz and wife Rose Lee.

Below: As former CEO, Bob volunteers at the Variety Club Telethon with employees of Wellmark Blue Cross Blue Shield.

Conservationist

In 2000, a dream was realized. Through the vision of three Iowans—Governor Robert Ray and Des Moines business leader Don Lamberti and Gerry Schnepf (opposite page), Keep Iowa Beautiful (KIB) was created with the purpose of instilling a sense of pride in Iowans through funding of beautification projects across Iowa's landscape. Today, KIB has raised tens of thousands of private and public dollars to fund hundreds of beautification projects across the state of Iowa—projects that Iowans and our state's visitors can enjoy and be proud of.

Left clockwise: Governor Ray with Don Lamberti (left) at a Keep Iowa Beautiful function. • Governor Ray leads the way with a broom as he and other dignitaries help maintain "the Cleanest Show in Town" at the Iowa State High School Girls Basketball Tournament. • Bob Ray with former KIB Board member Ed Skinner, U.S. Secretary of Agriculture and former Iowa Governor Tom Vilsack and Keep America Beautiful CEO Matt McKenna.

Right: Bob with Marshalltown mascot, "Cleaniac."

Below: Ray receiving the prestigious "Iowa" Award, with wife Billie, as Governors Branstad and Vilsack look on.

Photo credit: Loess Hills-Bob Buman

Photo credit: Mines of Spain-Gary Hamer

Photo credit: Prairie-Gary Tonhouse

Photo credit: Prairie-Jack Vanden Heuval

Photo credit: Spring Run Wetland-Daniel Ruf

Photo credit: Prairie-Jack Vanden Heuval

75

Photo credit: Mines of Spain-Gary Hamer

Photo credit: Prairie-Jack Vanden Heuval

Below and right: The John and Mary Pappajohn Sculpture Park, part of downtown Des Moines' Western Gateway redevelopment.

Photo credit: Des Moines Art Center/John and Mary Pappajohn Sculpture Park. Photography © Cameron Campbell; Integrated Studios

Photo credit: Des Moines Art Center/TH Painted Steel, Artist:
Mark diSuvero. Photography © Cameron Campbell; Integrated Studios

World Traveler

Africa

"Africa was a magnificent experience for Billie and me. The people were extremely friendly—and curious. They went out of their way to make us feel welcome and enjoyed being in front of the camera. The clothes and jewelry they wore were stunning and intricate in their detail."

"The peoples of Africa have wonderfully rich cultures and were extremely proud to display their tribal costumes and designs in every village we visited."

"The majestic creatures that roam the African continent were a true delight to see in person and up close."

"Everywhere we looked, there were opportunities to try and capture the vast beauty of Africa through the camera lens."

World Traveler

Bangkok

"One of the things that fascinated us the most about Bangkok was the marketplace. There were vendors busily selling their exotic (at least, to us) foods and other unique goods, while people milled about sampling and negotiating the price of all the food selections."

101

"The streets were filled with the high energy of day-to-day commerce and people out and about on their daily errands. The children seemed eager to meet these strangers from a place called 'America.'"

เขตอภัยทาน

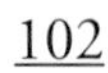

“This wall in Bangkok, adorned with these magnificent figures crafted with intricate detail and exquisite color, really caught my eye.”

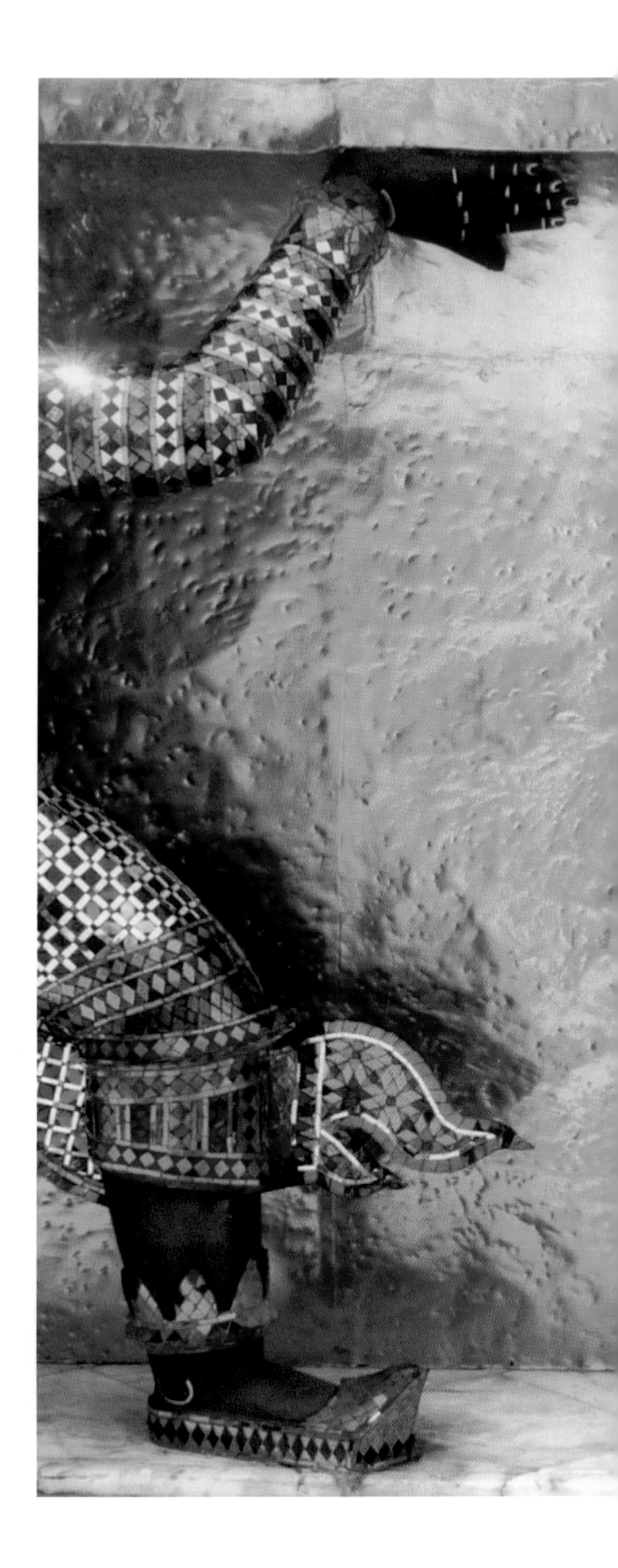

World Traveler

China

"China was one of the greatest trips we took with our family. The amazing people and the captivating backdrops were truly an experience we will never forget."

“The children were friendly and curious and a delight to be around. I happened to catch this bride-to-be in her beautiful gown on her way to her wedding.”

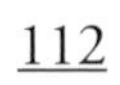

"The night lights in the city of Shanghai were amazing to behold. The colors were magnificent! All along the streets there were interesting people to see and we found ourselves taking every opportunity to soak in the culture . . . and snap memorable photos to bring back home."

"I found myself standing in the middle of Tiananmen Square among people from every corner of the globe. It's easy to be overwhelmed by the history that has taken place on this world stage."

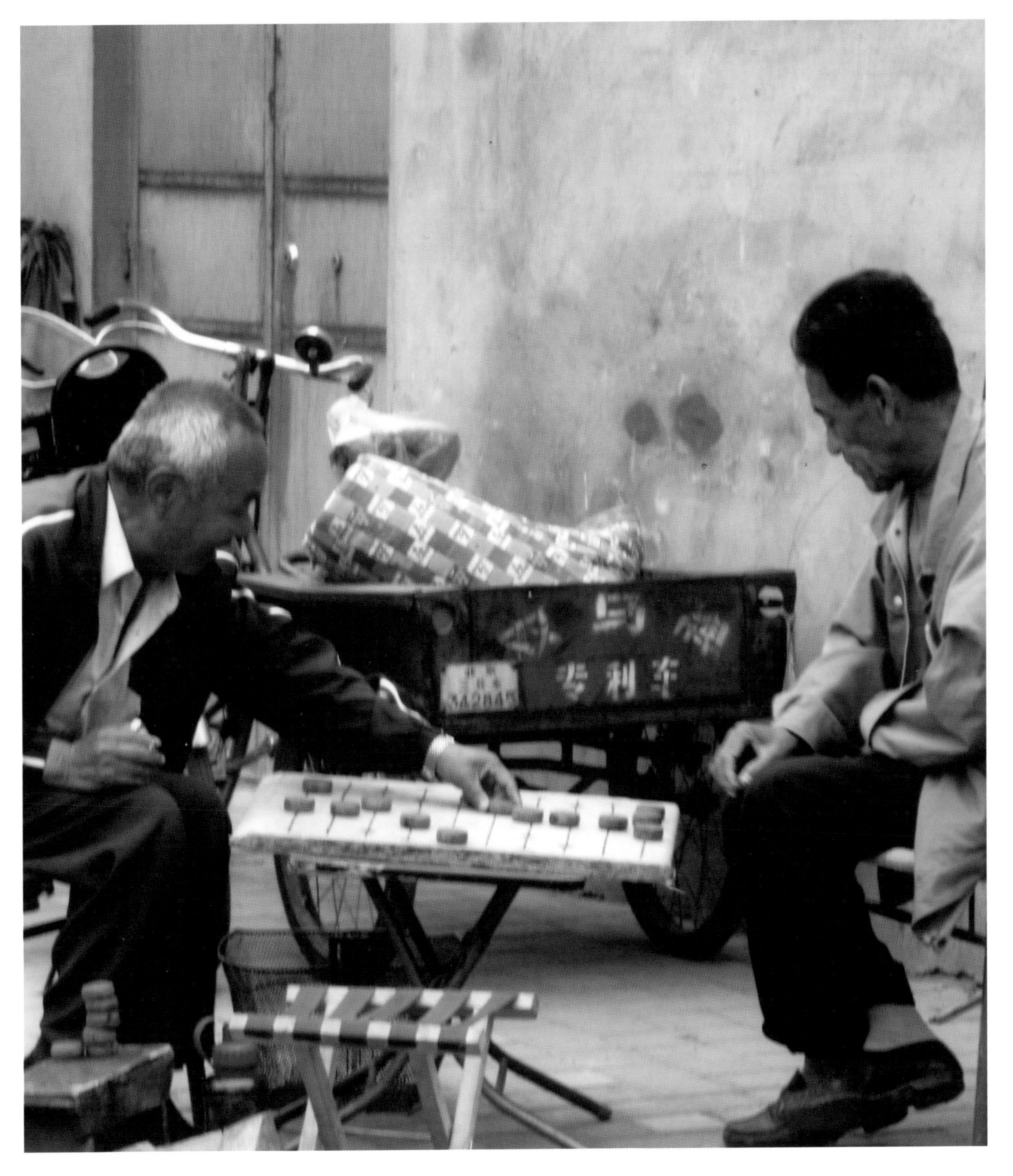
专利车

World Traveler

Egypt

“From the vast desert landscape to the remarkable architectural and physical feats of the pyramids, Egypt was an amazing adventure.”

World Traveler

Ireland

"Ireland was delightful from Day One. I felt myself wanting to capture the lush emerald hillside and rustic architecture filled with warm, wonderful characters deeply immersed in their endearing, colorful culture. No wonder people say, 'Everyone is an Irishman at heart.'"

World Traveler

Italy

"This was such an inspirational trip for us. To be able to see and experience even a small part of Italy's vast history of art and architecture was life-changing. It was as if the people themselves were subjects on a large art canvas."

FACTORY

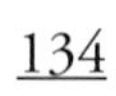

"Everywhere we looked you could feel history coming to life through all of the magnificent buildings and structures, many of them hundreds of years old or older."

World Traveler

London

"From Big Ben and the Houses of Parliament through the streets of London, it was a timeless lesson in the profound history of London. I found myself quite intrigued by viewing this colorful city from the unique perspective of its rooftops."

"The architecture and the rooftop perspective were fascinating to me. I especially found this bell tower atop a church quite interesting. It was like seeing childhood stories and history lessons coming to life."

In tribute to Robert D. Ray and in recognition of our generous contributors to the publication of this book.

Bob Ray's leadership, vision and compassion for people throughout the world are an inspiration to us all.

John and Janis Ruan Family

If you were to search for a proven role model for a Governor, a corporate CEO, a university president, or even a Mayor, one person would immediately qualify – Robert D. Ray. Through his leadership, integrity, vision and humanity, he has tirelessly served not only the people of Iowa, but those of the nation and the world.

Bill and Karla Fultz Family

In appreciation of Governor Ray's leadership and commitment to economic development and his work with Iowa's Rural Electric Cooperatives.

Iowa Area Development Group and IADG Community Foundation

Robert Ray and the late Marvin Pomerantz have been two of the most effective leaders in our state for more than four decades. Their relationship began in junior high, and their partnership was reestablished when Governor Ray first ran for office in 1968. The governor's and Mr. Pomerantz's impact on our state are examples of the many good things a public-private partnership can achieve. As Iowans, we are all beneficiaries of that partnership . . . and their service.

Marvin A. and Rose Lee Pomerantz

Hy-Vee has been honored to share Iowa's stage with one of Iowa's treasures, Bob Ray.

Ray works tirelessly on issues — education, the environment, health and wellness, character development — critical to Iowans and important to all Americans. Hy-Vee supports initiatives and charities for children, numerous community improvement projects across the Midwest, and an ongoing effort to make Iowa the healthiest state in America.

His commitment to keeping Iowa beautiful — and this project, chronicling his life and travels for generations to come — stands out as truly admirable.

Hy-Vee, Inc.

"I can't think of anyone who has better served the people of Iowa, in his many important roles, as Bob Ray. A true leader in every way."

William C. Knapp

This book is a powerful tribute to Governor Ray and demonstrates the vast impact he has had in Iowa and throughout the world. Generations to come will now be able to learn more about his tremendous legacy that has changed our state forever.

Tom Aller
President, Interstate Power and Light – Alliant Energy

Alliant Energy

Bob Ray and Don Lamberti both realized the need to create a program that would educate the public about illegal dumping, littering, and grafitti on Iowa's highways and the importance of beautifying our communities. They formed Keep Iowa Beautiful in 2000 and affiliated it with Keep America Beautiful. Today it has become a major factor in helping realize their original goal. We pay tribute to both Bob and Don in this wonderful book.

Casey's General Stores

Kitty and I are so pleased to be included in supporting this book that helps keep Iowa a beautiful place. Its people and its land interact with each other to make an enduring combination of the highest quality of life and living. We are proud to honor this man who has served this cause and so many others for the benefit of all Iowans.

Tom and Kitty Stoner

Through a remarkable life, Governor Ray transcended mere politics and position. He led with civility, kindness and innovation. His legacy is truly making a difference in people's lives.

The Principal Financial Group

This book was made possible by the following contributors:

Alliant Energy Company

Bob and Gloria Burnett

Casey's General Stores

Bill and Karla Fultz Family

Bob and Diane Greenlee

In Memory of Howard Gregory

E. David Hurd

Hy-Vee, Inc.

Iowa Area Development Group/IADG Community Foundation

Iowa State Bar Association

Sam and Lori Kalainov

Gary Kirke

William C. Knapp

Dimaggio Nichols

David Oman

Pioneer Communications/*The Iowan* Magazine

Marvin A. and Rose Lee Pomerantz

The Principal Financial Group

Ed Redfern

Stan and Jody Reynolds

John and Janis Ruan Family

Tom and Kitty Stoner

Strategic America

Ted Townsend

Alan Zuckert

Book Design: Pat Fultz, Fultz Design
Book Editor: Mark Lunde

Prairie Meadows is proud to partner with Keep Iowa Beautiful in offering this educational gift to more than 500 public libraries across Iowa through a community betterment grant from Prairie Meadows.

Through this gesture, we hope to help preserve the life work of Governor Ray in making our world a better and brighter place.

Prairie Meadows is a non-profit corporation licensed by the State of Iowa doing business in the gaming, entertainment and lodging industries.

Since 1995, Prairie Meadows has given more than $1 billion through taxes, grants and charitable donations to the people of Iowa. More than $500 million of this funding has promoted economic development, agriculture, jobs and tourism.

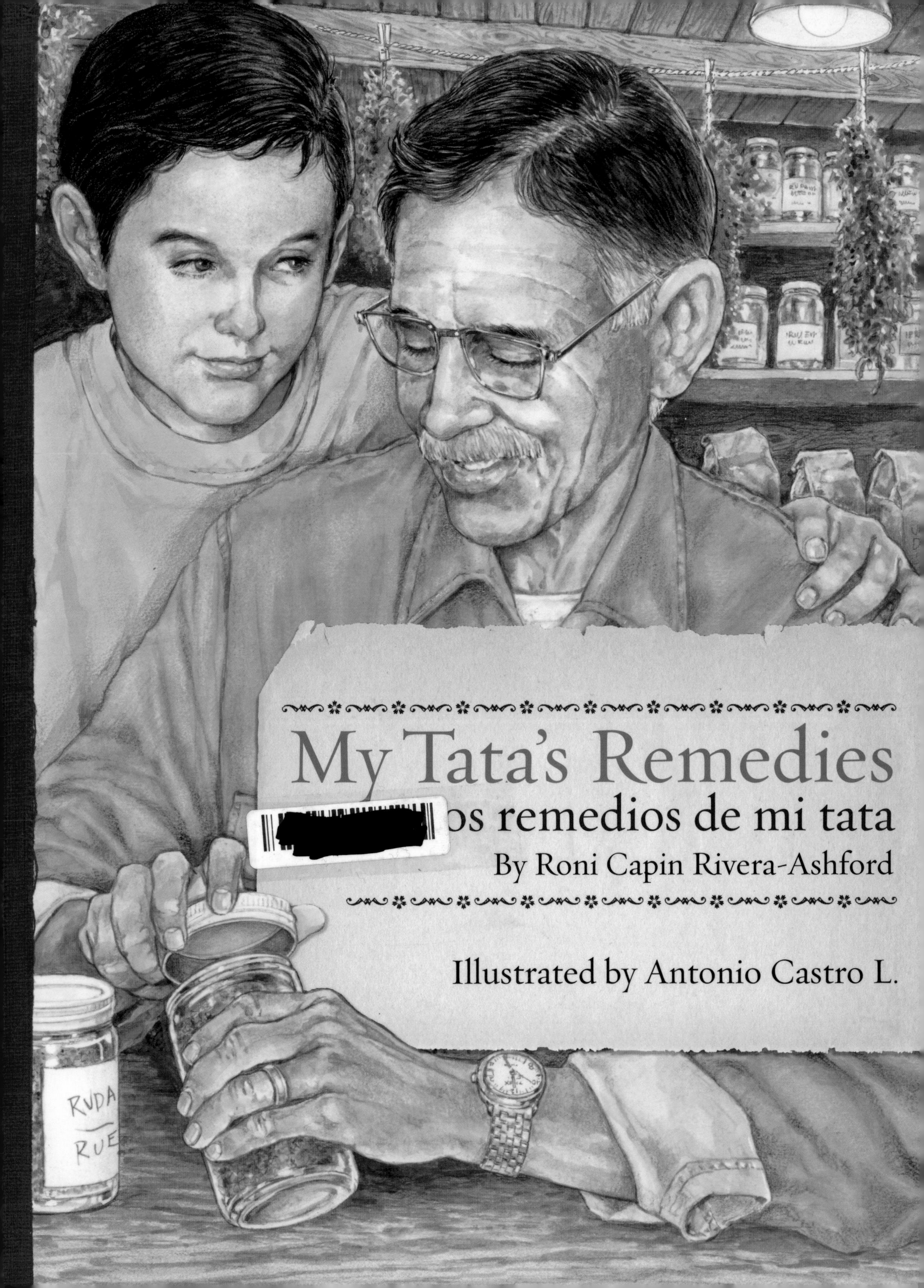
My Tata's Remedies
os remedios de mi tata
By Roni Capin Rivera-Ashford
Illustrated by Antonio Castro L.
RUDA
RUE